Moving
Forward

MOVING FORWARD

Poems from My Journey
toward Inner Healing

Ikiea Sherry

XULON PRESS

Xulon Press
2301 Lucien Way #415
Maitland, FL 32751
407.339.4217
www.xulonpress.com

Unless otherwise indicated, Scripture quotations taken from the King James Version (KJV) – *public domain*.

Printed in the United States of America.

ISBN-13: 978-1-63221-742-4

Dedication

To my mother, Deborah Lynn Sherry, my sisters,
Shani Sherry, Shaquan Dye and Joia Sherry

To countless women friends and mentors who
have been instrumental in the shaping of my life.

For those women who choose to walk
with God on your healing journey.

"Beloved, I wish above all things that thou mayest
prosper and be in health, even as thy soul prospereth."
3 John 1:2 (KJV)

ACKNOWLEDGEMENTS

I would like to thank Dr Kaye Hardee for first encouraging me to share these poems to minister to other people. God has used you as one of the key instruments in my healing journey. Thank you for the time and countless hours we have spent together during my healing process.

I thank Rev. Gary L. Lemons as the editor of this book and a great source of encouragement during this writing process. Your expertise and time given to this project have been invaluable. Thank you for seeing the impact this book can have on the lives of hurting women.

I would like to thank my sister Shani Sherry, who was inspired to write the Foreword for this book. I thank you for encouraging me to open my mouth and speak how I feel. Thank you for the years we have lived together and helped one another to grow in our relationships with the Lord. Thank you for being my accountability partner and the iron that sharpens iron in my life. Thank you for always being honest with me, even when it hurts.

To the Sherry family—including my father, mother, sisters, brother-in-law, niece and nephews—I thank each of you for your love and support. Each of you has had a significant influence on the woman I am today. Your words, tears, pain, memories, and laughter have helped inspire me to write this book.

Thank you, Lord Jesus my Savior for redeeming me. Your love truly never fails.

To my God and Father, I thank you for the doors you have opened in my life. Thank you for putting me in positions and places I never expected to be. Thank you for using me in spite of my faults, failures, hang ups, and issues. I want to thank you Father, for your patience and love to see me through this delicate healing process. You and you alone are the One who can make good out the pain and ashes of my life. Thank you for not allowing any of my tears, pain, frustration, rejection, or hurt to be wasted.

TABLE OF CONTENTS

Foreword xi
Introduction xiii
My Journals: Pouring out My Heart xvii

POEMS FROM MY JOURNEY

"My Beautiful Scar" 3
"I Am A Tree" 5
"Move Forward" 7
"Scared Little Girl" 9
"Symptoms" 11
"The Healer" 13
"The Woman Within" 15
"I Belong to God" 17
"Today" 19
"The Chain Breaker" 21
"Bring Me Back" 23
"Where Do I Go from Here?" 25
"Transformation" 27
"Words of My Heart" 29
"The Monster Within" 31
"Food" 33
"Addiction" 35
"Shame" 37
"Fear" 39
"Buffet" 41
"Holding My Daddy's Hand" 43
"People's Voices" 45

About the Author 47

FOREWORD

TEACHING HIGH SCHOOL LITERATURE HAS TAUGHT me this: students-hate-poetry. In fact, many people do stating that it has uncommon punctuation, weird sentences, and no meaning. In my classes, armed with this understanding, I begin with the poetry unit. I do not start with a poem or list of poetry terms, but I open with a news video of a tragedy.

On April 16, 2007, Virginia Tech experienced the fatal massacre of 32 of its students and faculty. It is marked as the deadliest school shooting in US history. The incident was reported with cell phone footage of gunshots by terrified bystanders themselves. I need students to understand the panic and horror of such an incident, though violent. I must place them there. My students were children of ages 5 and 6 during the incident. They would not have understood such tragedy.

I stop the video. Silence and shock. I broadcast the memorial service. The dome is filled with distraught mourners: tears, brokenness, fear, devastation, emptiness, and hopelessness fill its seats. Then Nikki Giovanni rises to the podium and recites her poem "We are Virginia Tech." Within 2 minutes she stirred this solemn assembly to applause. They chanted their fight song. Even my students clap.

That is the power of poetry. It can move souls from pain to hope to strength. But it all begins with an event. Poetry is the person's response to the event. It is a pronouncement or protest if you will of the soul. It says it happened. I saw it. I was struck. It mattered. I am alive.

In this book, my sister Ikiea, has cornered the events in her life's journey and penned her pronouncement of them. May your soul be moved to hope as you read this book and walk your own journey of healing. Shani Sherry

INTRODUCTION

"Limping, hurting I run back to You; right where I left
You patiently waiting for me. Crying and ashamed, I
find my way back to You. You hold me and comfort
me as You carry me through this painful lesson. This
same old familiar pattern You have walked me through.
I'm walking next to You again. I'm holding my Daddy's
hand as You walk with me through this meadow on the
path of my life once again."

Ikiea Sherry
Excerpt from my poem, "Holding My Daddy's Hand"

I HAVE REACHED A TIME IN MY LIFE WHERE THE COST
of continuing to linger in emotional pain has become more than I can
bear. Releasing myself from the weight of it has allowed me to experi-
ence the joy of self-recovery. I am no longer willing to pay the soul-de-
stroying price the burden of emotional pain has cost me. In the poems
which compose this book, I have determined to write myself back into
being—inspired by the Holy Spirit guiding every word in every poem
you will read. As each one represents my path toward freedom, let the
loving Spirit in each inspire you on your journey toward God's destiny
for your self-liberation and inner healing.

Healing Journey

I invite you to walk through this healing journey with me as you
read through the poems in this book. May you be helped and empow-
ered to take your own healing journey. I pray these poems will help you

to express the pain that you have been running away from. I encourage you to take the journey on your road to your own inner healing. Allow the Lord to sweetly, gently, yet firmly walk with you every step of the way through your own internal healing process.

To enable you to experience my journey toward freedom through the life-saving power of the Holy Spirit, first allow me to share my life's story of inner and outer healing.

Going Back, Where It All Began

I believe God has given me the gift of poetry, maybe because this is His way of giving me a voice at a time that I really needed to find it. Poetry resonates with me because it is palatable, meaning everyone can read it. I can be anonymous and not have to disclose every detail of the events or situations that have happened in my life. It gives me the freedom to express thoughts about something without having to follow the rules of traditional, formal writing. Poetry represents freedom to me because I don't have to be under conventional literary constraints. I can be myself and not have to follow those rules. I have been and am struggling to be a person who has her own voice and will not continue to allow it to be stifled by my need for someone else's approval or need to control me.

As a source of biblical inspiration, I identify with the figure of Joshua. Joshua was a courageous man. He was faithful to God, a fighter/warrior, and a leader. He was someone who led and encouraged others to follow God. He and his family also encouraged others to follow God. I also relate to Joshua because he was someone who sought to follow the Lord and do what God called him to do in spite of other people's actions. He demonstrated fearlessness because the Lord told him not to be afraid, but be courageous.

I struggle with fear a lot, and I need the Lord's help to be courageous. I, like Joshua, desire to live a life that is pleasing to God. He did what

God sent him to do. God had a great work for Joshua to do. I also believe God has a great work for me to do, even though I don't know all the details. Like Joshua, I also find myself drawn to situations where I help people find their way to God or His will, despite the mess in their lives. It's like helping people put the broken pieces of their lives back together again—ultimately for God to receive the glory.

However, I am a recovering people pleaser. Stress, anxiousness, and fear were big parts of my life growing up. I was picked on a lot in school, so my response was that I just wanted to become invisible and not make any waves or problems with anyone wherever I went. My life felt out of control. As a result, I became insecure, shy, and very self-conscious. I turned to food as a way to manage my stress, but it also gave me something in my life that was under my control. As a result, however, becoming overweight made me feel ugly. I wasn't into athletics, nor did I possess a desire to play sports. In spite of this, I excelled academically. Becoming an outstanding student was the only way I felt significant.

Running Away

I spent many years trying to run from the pain of my life experiences. Rejection, fear, and feeling insignificant were just a few of the feelings at the root of my pain. Having to sit and listen to the discouraging thoughts in my head was hard to endure. It was easy to run to my addictions to distract me from having to listen to these thoughts or feelings. I became good at running away; anything to cover the pain I felt. In order to enter this process of inner healing, I had to stop running away and walk directly into my pain.

My Journals: Pouring out My Heart

THE WORDS OF MY HEART ARE POURED OUT ON PAGES of journals I never knew I needed. The poems in this book are like travel stamps from the places I've been on my journey through the process of spiritual and emotional healing. I used journals to document the pain and experiences of this journey of inner healing. This journey has been both difficult and challenging work and continues to be hard work. From my journal entries, I wrote poems to help express the flood and often difficult emotions that would arise when I would begin to revisit painful experiences from my past. Before I began writing poems in my journal, I never would have considered myself a writer, let alone a poet. These poems are the result of a very dark time in my life. They are composed of the words I've used to express the pain I medicated; the pain I stuffed down and hid; the pain I denied; the invisible constant companion I refused to acknowledge.

Washing Machine

Clean clothes are a necessity. For some people, based on their station in life, having clean clothes is a privilege that many of us take for granted. To put on fresh clean clothes is a privilege. To have a washing machine to wash my clothes is a luxury. I feel as if I've been in the washing machine of healing for so very long. Pain, fear, addiction, depression, and loneliness are a few of the issues of my life that have so soiled my soul. God is washing these things out of me. Around and around I go being washed in God's Word as He makes me clean. Sometimes I'm jostled and turned upside down and inside out, just like clothes in a washing machine. But this washing machine of a healing process is just what I need.

The blood of my Lord and Savior Jesus Christ was my initiation into this inner washing process, my sanctification. Slowly but surely, I'm being shaped in His image. This washing process removes those things in me that are not like Him.

I've heard that the spin cycle is the longest cycle on a washing machine. Clothes are spun at high rates of speed to wring out as much water as possible. Pain, fear, shame, food addiction, depression, and other issues are all being wrung out of me. Surgeries on my body, counseling sessions, family changes, my spiritual growth, my relationship with the Lord, and the experience of His forgiveness have all been tools the Lord has used to help wash me clean.

I invite you to read this book to begin the journey of your own healing process, wherever it may lead you. One step in front of the other, hand in hand with our loving God and Father. Obey the voice of our Father as He beacons you—*come dear child, come.*

POEMS FROM MY JOURNEY

"My Beautiful Scar"

You are six and a quarter inches long with spots on the sides; reminders of the staples that first held you closed.

You were not what I expected when I awoke from my couple hours of sleep. A smile, not a half of a ruler, was all I expected to see.

You've made your home right down the middle of my stomach; starting just below and off center of my navel.

I see you every day when I look in the mirror, long and dark staring back at me. How ugly you were at first to me. I didn't have eyes to see what you would yet come to be.

My eyes are opened now. No longer are you ugly or a shock to me. I've had time of reflection and healing. I've experienced a change in my feelings.

You are my testimony because through you God healed me.

You are my answered prayer because you showed me that God heard my cry.

You are my token to remind me that God is faithful to keep his promises.

You are my Beautiful Scar.
IDS 12/16/10

"I Am A Tree"

I am a tree with withered leaves – shrunken from the life being drawn out of me.

I am a tree with cracked branches – splintered by people snatching fruit from me.

I am a tree with peeling bark – shedding from acidic soil spoiling my roots.

I am tree with a bent trunk – crooked from unsteady stakes supporting me.

The husbandman came and tended to me.
He tilled and plowed and turned the soil.
He staked and tied and shored my trunk.
He trimmed and bound and healed my branches.

I am a tree with bright green leaves.
I am a tree with plentiful fruit
My fruit is valued because the husbandman guards it.
Since the husbandman came, I am a tree full of life with an unlimited source of nutrients from Him.
I AM A TREE.
IDS 5/13/11

"Move Forward"

Although the pain of life has cemented your feet to the ground, move forward.

Although the memories of your past cause you to cover your face in shame, move forward.

Although the road ahead seems dim, dark and blue, move forward.

Although the fear of failure has you gripped tightly in its grasp, move forward.

Although your time to reach your goal is not yet clear or known, move forward.

God has a plan made just for you that can only be fulfilled by you, if you would only,
MOVE FORWARD.
IDS 5/25/11

"Scared Little Girl"

Scared little girl hiding away from the world with its loud noises and crowded streets full of angry shouting people going nowhere.

Scared little girl hiding in shame from the things your little eyes were never supposed to see, your little hands were never supposed to touch, and your little mind was never supposed to know.

Scared little girl longing to be seen, loved and be called Daddy's little girl with your round body and round face.

Scared little girl hiding yourself away because you never fit in other children's games blocking out their jokes and jeers.

Scared little girl come out of hiding now. The Comforter, your Helper and Protector has come. The Lord Jesus has come to set you free.
IDS 5/31/11

"Symptoms"

Symptoms are present; they show up when something is wrong. They are diverse. They come in all types of forms.

Symptoms are resilient. They pop up over and over again...

Symptoms are evidence of sin. They let us know there are problems within us.

Symptoms will never go away until you deal with the problem. You have to find out the root of the problem.

No need to fear, the Great Physician is here. The Healer has finally come.

Open up and let Him in. He's come not to heal the symptoms, but the problem within.
IDS 6/22/11

"The Healer"

My condition is severe. My heart's been broken and my thoughts are far from Him.

My condition is serious. My behavior is sinful and I've no desire to change.

My condition is sad. My countenance is lonely and depressed. Joy is not within me.

The Healer has come. I've showed Him my condition. No more denial, hiding, or running.

The Healer has come. I've told Him all about who I am. He's made His diagnosis and in recovery, here I am.

Healer do what only You can do. Fix, change, repair, restore, correct, and redirect what only You can.
Fix me Healer, fix me.
IDS 6/29/11

"The Woman Within"

The woman within is held captive by fear; chained by doubt and gagged by depression.

The woman within is riddled with guilt from the habits and sins that plague her life.

The woman within is broken by the failures and rejection she has known.

The woman within wants to be set free; she wants to have joy and be made whole.

Oh woman within, there's hope for you. It's found in the Lover of your soul.

Oh woman within open wide your heart; open wide your hands. Open wide, open wide, open wide...
the Healer, the Wonderful Counselor, the Prince of Peace, the Mighty God, the Lover of your soul has come.
IDS 7/18/11

"I Belong to God"

To God I am accepted.
To God I am loved and enough all on my own.
To God I don't have to perform to be approved by Him.

I am His.

To God I am unique, a one of a kind.
To God I am priceless.
To God I was worth the death of His son.
I belong, I belong, I belong to God.
IDS 8/22/11

"Today"

Today is all the time I'm given; tomorrow is not promised to me.
Today is all that I can see. I don't know the future.
Today is all the provision I need; tomorrow can take care of itself.
Today is all the concern I can handle; tomorrow has its own troubles.
Today is a gift that's been given to me, not to be squandered or taken lightly.

Today is all I have. What am I going to do with it?
IDS 11/16/11

"The Chain Breaker"

Behind a prison cell chained to the wall, I could see the world in front of me.

Hopes, opportunities, dreams all beckoning me to get free; beckoning me to take hold of what I've been missing out on.

As much as I desired, as much as I tried, I couldn't get free. So in time, I've settled for cheap substitutions—never ever giving me what I desired.

These chains have hindered me from moving and thinking and even dreaming. These chains have slowly choked the life out of my hope to be free.

A visitor came to my cell one day and assessed my condition. He saw me bound and lifeless and without hope. I had no more fight to be free.

That visitor came and never left. By my side is where He remains— talking to me, helping me, giving me hope, and new life.

One by one, the chains of my life are breaking and falling away. My visitor has come to stay. Slowly, patiently, gently, yet firmly—He works to free me. He didn't leave me the way He found me, but He chose to set me free.

Hopes, opportunities, dreams and new life—I see them as possibilities now. No longer am I behind that prison cell. I'm crawling, walking and running free in the hands of the visitor that came to see me.

Who is He you ask? Jesus Christ is He—my Savior, my Helper, my Life, my Hope, and my Healer.
The Chain Breaker is He.
IDS 12/02/11

"Bring Me Back"

Again, I set off in a direction headed to achieve the plan I thought I heard from you.

I'm fearful, doubting, anxious, and confused. Did I really hear what you said? Is this really what you wanted me to do? I'm questioning, seeking and looking for clarity from you. Please Lord—bring me back.

Again, I've charged ahead of you leaving you behind. Not knowing the way. I'm lost one more time. Please Lord—bring me back.

Help me Lord to grab your hand and follow where you lead me. I don't know the way. I don't know the full plan. Please Lord—bring me back.

Bring me back to my place by your side, walking hand in hand with you.

Bring me back to that place of quiet peace, as I trust in your loving care.

Bring me back to a place of clarity and vision of your plan.

Bring me back to the path where you're on and we're walking hand-in-hand.
Please Lord—bring me back.
IDS 6/11/12

"Where Do I Go from Here?"

I'm looking around wondering where to go. How far to run? Where to stop? Which road to take?
Where do I go from here?

Regrets behind me, fear in front of me, indecision on either side. All I can ask, all I can say is, "Where do I go from here?"

If I stay here, my dreams are going to die; suffocated by doubt and hindered by my paralyzed state. Where do I go from here?

My future calls and beckons me forward, calling me to come follow in the path of a future unknown, despite the fear and unclear site. Where do I go from here?
IDS 10/18/12

"Transformation"

No longer am I a little girl manipulated and having to do as I'm told. No longer am I a little girl unable to control my surroundings or voice my opinion.
I am a Woman.

No longer am I a teenager with limited responsibilities, limited resources, and limited options.
I am a Woman.

No longer am I a young adult learning the work force and forging a new independent life for myself.
I am a Woman.

No longer do I have to struggle to believe, accept, and define myself as how others have chosen to categorize me.
I am a Woman.

No longer do I have to allow myself to care for people, decisions, circumstances, or consequences that are NOT my own.
I am a Woman.

I am a Woman who can think and make a decision and stick to it; not out of fear or obligation, but because I can.

I am a Woman who can take care of the needs and responsibilities that are my own; not because I'm told to, but because I am capable, competent, and experienced.

I am a Woman who can define myself by who God says I am. I am not bound to people's opinions or thoughts of me; not of my own definition of who I should be, but because I can fully embrace the design of the One who created me.

I am not a little girl.

I am not a teenager.

I am not a young adult.

I AM A WOMAN.
IDS 5/11/13

"Words of My Heart"

The words of my heart have been poured out on pages of journals I never knew I needed.

The words of my heart have given a voice to the emotions, attitudes, and dreams of my heart. I've learned to use words in new ways; ways to shout, speak, and release what's in my heart.

I no longer have to allow words to shackle me based on labels others have given me. I no longer have to be bound by the names of things I've done.

Words have become a way for me to express the healing going on in my heart. My words can be used to build up others and tear down walls in my own heart.

The words of my heart are poured out on pages of journals I never knew I needed. These words have helped me express to God what I bottled up inside.
He can handle these words, these labels, these names, these disappointments, these fears, these dreams, and my guilt.

The words of my heart are poured out on pages of journals I never knew I needed. These words have been received by my gracious, forgiving, loving Savior who encourages me to speak them.

The words of my heart are poured out on pages of journals I never knew I needed. The words of my heart have given me a voice now in a way I didn't know was there. I can speak now. I can speak now to the audience of One who hears me.

The words of my heart are poured out on pages of journals I never knew I needed.
IDS 6/11/13

"The Monster Within"

The monster within me is always crying out for more...more anger, more hurt, more depression, and more offenses.

The monster within me never rests...always moving around seeking for places where it can show its ugly head.

The monster within me started out small and innocent; if there is such a thing as an innocent monster. I fed it my pain, my hurt, my anger, and all my sarcastic comebacks whenever I was offended or ridiculed.

The monster within me is too big to handle now. I can't keep him it locked away and hidden. It comes out on its own now, unrestrained and hungry. It doesn't even eat the same food any more.

The monster within me eats <u>rage</u> now. Offenses are meals not snacks. Hurt and pain are what it craves. Depression is what it uses to wash it all down.

I can't carry this monster within me anymore. I'm tired, weary, and frustrated. I'm frustrated at this monster within me; this monster that I created. I'm too tired to keep it locked up and too weary to keep tying the chains it keeps breaking loose from.

Who will help deliver me from this monster within me; this monster that refuses to go?

Lord Jesus, help me, save me, deliver me, and free me from this monster that I created!
IDS 7/2/13

"Food"

I like the way it smells. I like the way it tastes. It comes in so many varieties and flavors. I like food.

I like the way it feels in my mouth. I love the different textures. I love food.

It's my drug of choice; my "something to ease the pain." It dulls the pain I feel when I'm all alone. It keeps me from having to think about my problems or my fears or my failures or my whatever. Food is my drug.

It's been my companion since I was a child; always available in whatever quantity I wanted. It's been my comfort when I've been rejected. It's never turned me down. Food is my friend.

It has consumed me now. It has filled all my empty places. I take up more space and weigh more because of it. It no longer brings comfort now. It acts more like an enemy. I struggle to break free of it. Food is my addiction.

I've met a new friend now. He brings comfort like I've never known. I can never get enough of Him. I eat of His love, His grace, His mercy, His forgiveness, His healing, and whatever else He offers. I can eat and eat and eat with no adverse reactions.

My Friend is my Savior, Jesus Christ, the lover of My Soul. He is my new addiction and always will be.
IDS 5/19/14

"ADDICTION"

Addiction is a crutch and barrier that prevents me from healing. It prevents me from feeling the weight of the pain I so desperately run from.

Addiction is like a pill used to manage headaches. It only deadens the pain for a while until it all comes rushing back.

Addictions are like weeds. They start small and continue to grow; larger and larger choking the life out of everything in their path.

My addictions started out as little bits of comfort to manage the pain of a desperate and fearful little girl. But now, my addictions have grown to overtake me; second rate options that never satisfy.

My addictions don't bring comfort anymore, only bondage. I'm like a slave working to satisfy a cruel task master; it can never be done.

I remember now that there's only One who can break the chains of addictions. There's only One who can set me free from the all-consuming need to satisfy them.

I remember that I am a child of the Chain Breaker; the One who can break the yoke of these addictions on my life.

Chain Breaker at your feet I lay the bondage of these addictions. I welcome your healing and freedom now!!!
IDS 5/19/14

"Shame"

Shame is the gloomy cloud that hangs over my head. It darkens the world all around me.

Shame is the heavy blanket that covers me from head to toe. It causes me to hide away.

Shame is the fog that limits my vision when I drive. I can hardly see a thing.

Shame is the obstacle that keeps me from living. I don't want to try or start new things.

Shame is the road block that blocks my path. It prevents me from making progress on the journey God has set for me.

Shame is heavy, like a boulder on my back.

Shame tarnishes. It steals my reflection.

Shame forces me into darkness.

Shame taunts me for the sin I've done. It reminds me of my wrong.

Who can deliver me from this shame I wear?

Jesus Christ the Messiah is the only One who can!
IDS 2/3/14

"Fear"

FEAR is like a second layer of skin. Everywhere I turn, every move I make, FEAR is always with me.

How do I remove this unwanted layer of skin? It's like pimples on my face; it won't go away.

I hide away because of it, lying under a cover of depression. I don't take risks and every opportunity brings failure in my mind.

My thinking is shackled by this FEAR. Will I ever have this, or will I ever have that? Will I ever be this, or will I ever be that? These are the questions that plague me.

Lord God, the only One who can change circumstances, lives, hearts and minds; please remove this FEAR from me. This worn, tattered cover I don't want to wear anymore.

Help me to know your perfect LOVE that will cast out all of my FEAR. Your LOVE never judges me, only accepts me. Your LOVE corrects me, never ridicules me. Your LOVE is overflowing and freely given, never held for ransom based on my performance.

LOVE me, LOVE me, LOVE me. My Father LOVE me. Help me to drink of your endless LOVE that will never leave me empty or full of fear! IDS 6/13/14

"Buffet"

I am a buffet. I've many entrées, appetizers, salads, and desserts to choose from. I've ample portions in mind, body, and soul. Conversation, personality, and style are all on the buffet too.

There are several types of people. Those who can appreciate buffets always come back for more. Never dissatisfied and always wanting more. They are intoxicated by what the buffet has to offer. They never mess over the food and always are sure to clean their plates.

There are some people who don't frequent buffets. Buffets are much too much to handle. Restaurant menus and snack machines are the only places these people will eat. Menu items and snacks are all they feel they need. Buffets don't appeal to them at all.

Then there are people who are under cover buffet lovers. On the outside they like to be known as those who frequent restaurants and snack machines. But, on the inside, they love buffets. They hang out at buffets when the crowd they want to impress isn't looking.

On the other hand, there are others who openly frequent buffets, but they mess over the food; never learning to fully appreciate all the buffet has to offer. Therefore, they are always missing out on all the benefits they could have had.

I'm a buffet. I have a lot to offer. I have to be careful of who I allow to partake of me, because not everyone can handle all that I have to give. Not everyone can appreciate all of me—mind, body, and soul. All buffet lovers are welcomed here.

I am a Buffet.

IDS 12/26/13

"Holding My Daddy's Hand"

It's been a long time since I've imagined us walking together in the meadow; my hand in yours as you lead me down the path of my life.

I see butterflies and tall wispy grass while we walk. I feel the sun shine on my face. Beautiful crisp clean air fills my nose. I feel such peace as we walk together.

I look to my left and something's caught my eye. I run towards it, captivated by it as I leave you behind. It's grabbed my attention and has my total focus in its grasp.

You stand there right where I left You as You watch me run away. This same old familiar pattern you've seen me do over and over again. Yet, You're patiently lovingly waiting for me.

The thing that's caught my eye was not at all what it appeared. It's full of pain, not beauty. I'm deceived yet again. Like prickly sandspurs, it's hard to get away from it.

Limping, hurting I run back to you; right where I left you patiently waiting for me. Crying and ashamed I find my way back to You. You hold me and comfort me as You carry me through this painful lesson. This same old familiar pattern you've walked me through.

I'm walking next to you again. I'm holding my Daddy's hand as you walk with me through this meadow on the path of my life once again.

Thank you, Daddy, my Lord.
IDS 6/10/14

"People's Voices"

People's voices are loud and demanding. They give their opinions when they're not wanted.

People's voices are confusing and misleading. They point you in directions you don't want to go.

People's voices are well intended. But they don't know what's best for you.

People's voices are like crowded thoughts. You just want to escape them.

God's voice is still and soft. His voice draws you to Him.

God's voice is sure and full of purpose. He knows exactly where He is leading you.

God's voice is consistent and peaceful. You can always count on what He says.

Let God's voice be your sure, steady guide. He's got great plans for where He's taking you. IDS 8/27/20

ABOUT THE AUTHOR

IKIEA SHERRY IS A NATIVE OF TAMPA, FL AND CUR-
rently resides in the Tampa Bay area. She has both B.S. and M.S. degrees
in Computer Science from Clark Atlanta University in Atlanta, GA.
She also has an M.B.A. degree in General Business. She is the leader
of a single women's life group at her local church. She continues to
pursue creative writing to encourage believers in their journey toward
inner healing.

I will lift up mine eyes unto the hills, from whence cometh my help.
My help *cometh* from the LORD, which made heaven and earth.
Psalm 121: 1 – 2 (KJV)

"When our Father has given us a message to share with those in need
of self-enlightenment and healing, He will always send a messenger of
hope. Ikiea Sherry's creative expressivity in this missionary work invites
readers to embark upon a path with her filled with the light of healing
through the life-saving power of Divine love." Dr. Gary L. Lemons

"Ikiea's poetic prose is beautifully unique. She writes expressions using
the wide spectrum of vulnerablity; from despair to hope, from depres-
sion to victory, and from sorrow to joy. Even the order in which the
poems were written, one can easily connect and follow Ikiea's journey
of dealing with her emotions while still leaning upon the love and peace
of her Heavenly Father. Well done, Ikiea." Jessica Bauchum

CPSIA information can be obtained
at www.ICGtesting.com
Printed in the USA
LVHW010526211220
674732LV00010B/329